I0177778

TM & copyright © by AMK Counseling 2017

All rights reserved.
Published in the United States by AMK Counseling
Chicago, IL

Visit us at
GritUpSeries.com
AMKCounseling.com

ISBN 978-0-9890102-45

Special thanks to the brain squad KH, KK & MV

Care to Repair

Helping children take responsibility for hurtful actions

Written by Abbie Kelley, MA, LCPC

Illustrated by Mary Kelley

Hi Jay, how was lunch?

It was good, except now Andre is upset with me and I don't know what to do.

What happened?

I'm kind of embarrassed...
I got caught lying.

I am sorry to hear that.
What happened?

Andre called to ask me to go to the park, but I didn't want to because it was too hot out.

So I blamed it on my mom and
said she wouldn't let me go out today.

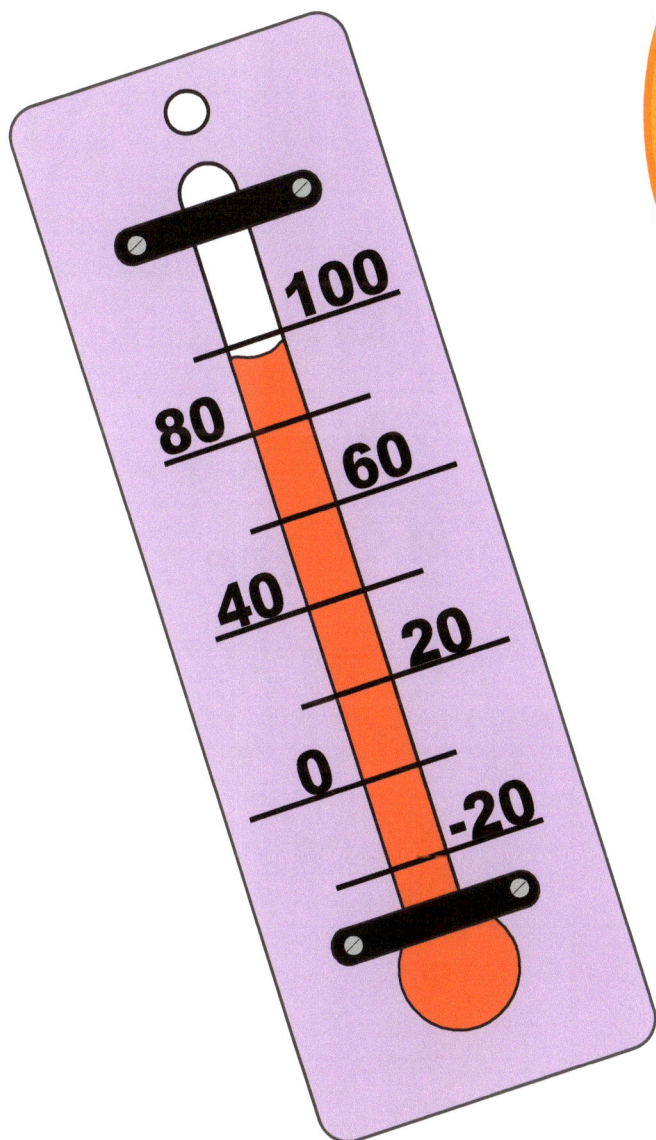

the BURGER shop

Later he saw me getting lunch with Victoria. He was so upset, he walked right by me without speaking to me. Now I don't know what to say to him.

Getting Gritty: Why do you think Jay did not tell Andre the truth?
When Andre saw Jay, how do you think Andre was feeling?

That is a dilemma. When we wrong someone or hurt their feelings (even if we didn't mean to) we need to care enough to repair the relationship.

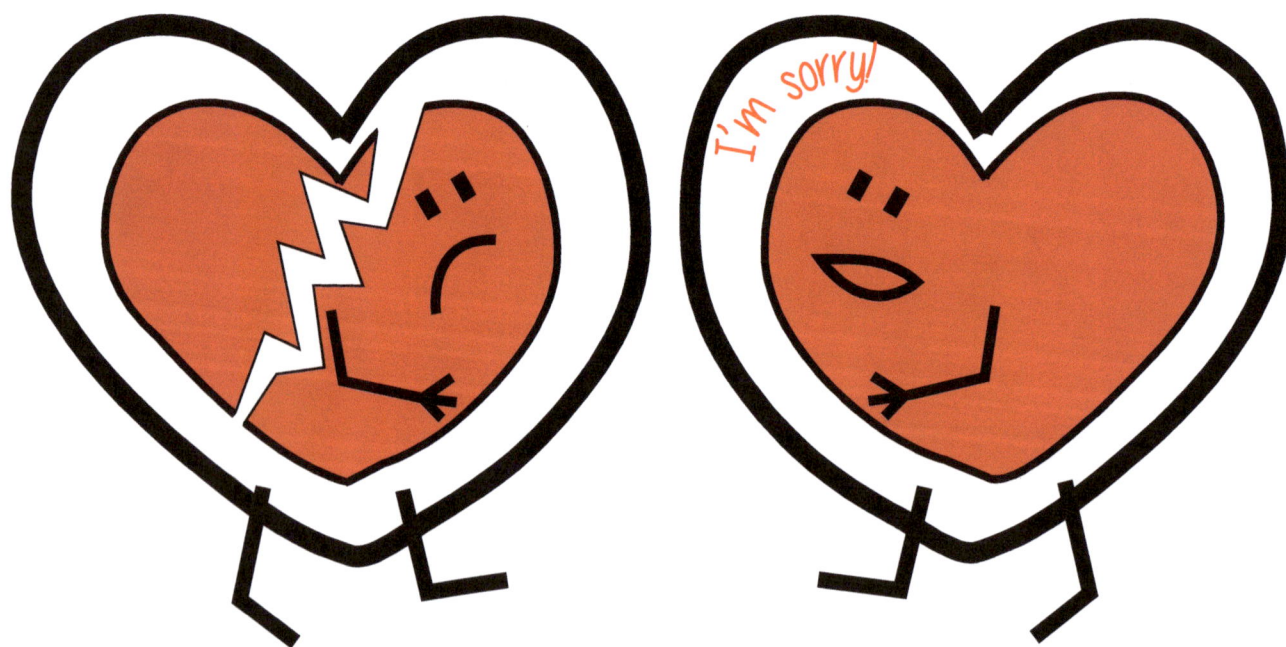

Like say "sorry"?

10

Yes, but saying "sorry" isn't enough. You have to repair the mistake or hurt you caused. It is difficult to do but necessary to help heal the hurt feelings.

Getting Gritty: When have you had to say "sorry" to someone? Why do you think apologizing can feel so uncomfortable?

It also helps people respect you and helps your relationships grow stronger.

There are 3 steps to take when you are working to repair a relationship.

Get ready, take a deep breath and have a sincere tone (you need to let others know you do care enough to repair).

CARE to REPAIR

1) Say you are sorry.

2) Take responsibility for what you are apologizing for.

3) State what you are willing to do to move forward.

Getting Gritty: Which step do you think is the most difficult?

14

If you take these steps, you can repair the wrong or the mistake you made to the relationship.

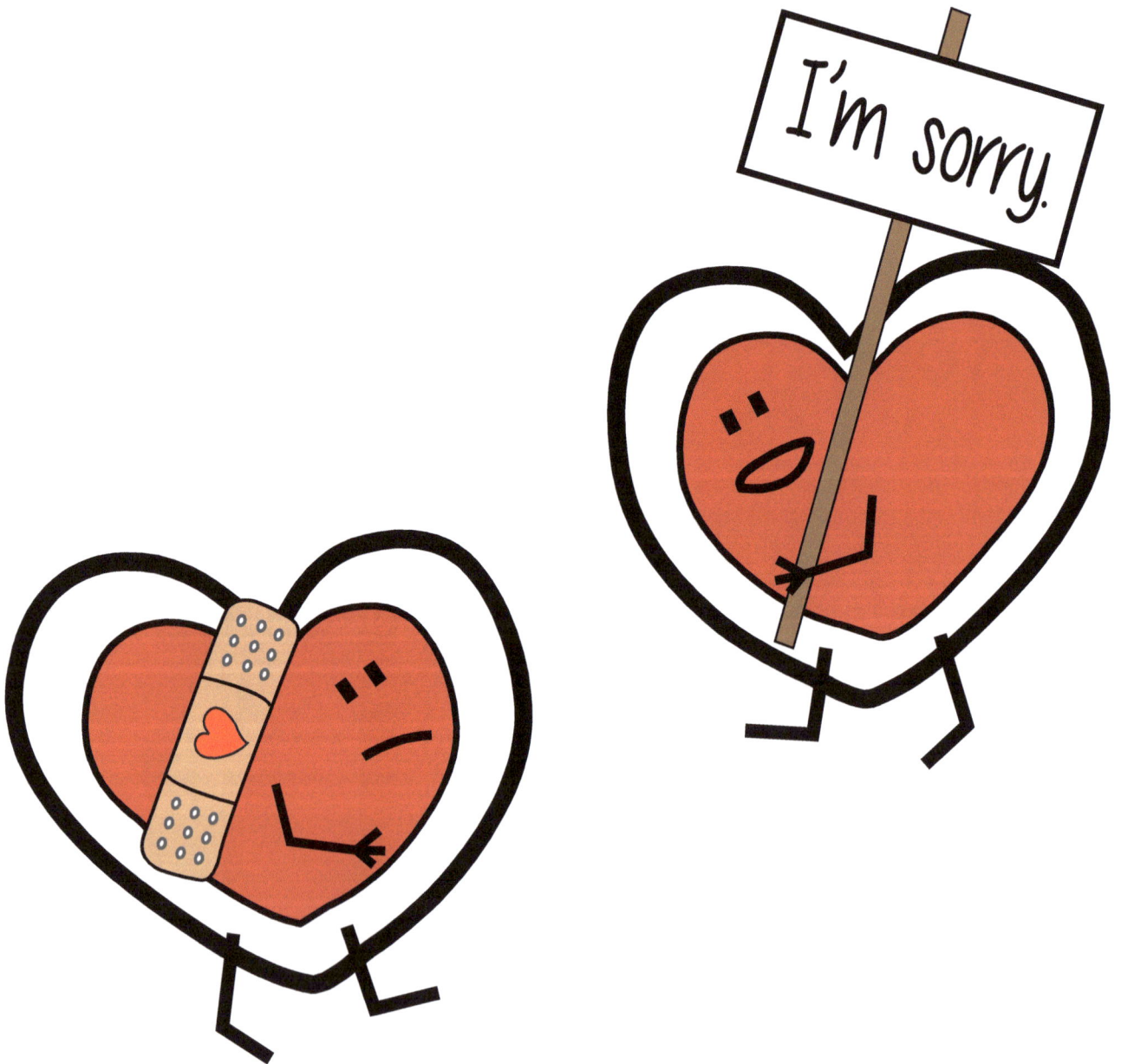

Some mistakes take more time
to work through, but it is worth
it for the people we care about.

Thanks, but I
need some time.

I'm sorry.

Of course I care enough to repair! Even though it is going to be difficult, I need to apologize.

I'm sorry about earlier. Can I come over so we can talk?

Umm, ok Jay. That would be fine.

Getting Gritty: Jay chose to talk to Andre face to face. Why do you think that was a better idea than talking on the phone or texting?

18

I'll say I am sorry I lied and hurt his feelings.

Then explain that I should have told him I wanted to hang out but it was too hot for the park.

Lastly, I'll say that I want to work on being honest with him in the future.

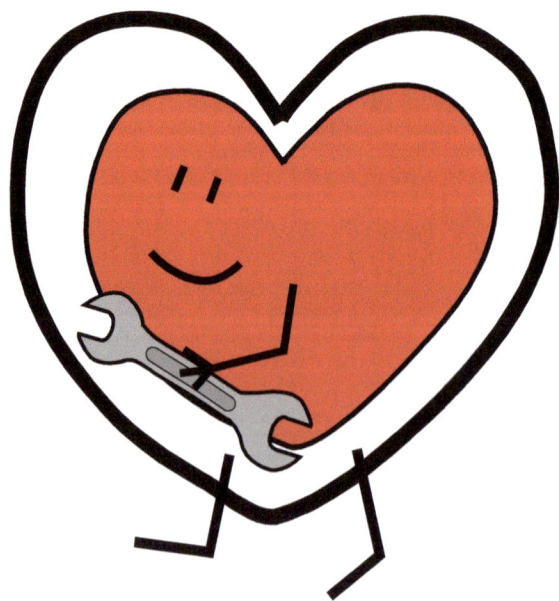

Sounds like you used all the steps.

☑ Say you are sorry.

☑ Take responsibility for what you are apologizing for.

☑ State what you are willing to do to move forward.

The next time this comes up it will be important to use **head and heart** communication to share your honest feelings.

It is important to learn from your mistakes and change your behavior. Otherwise people won't trust you and will be less willing to forgive you or grow the relationship.

I'm really sorry that I lied to you again!

Yeah... whatever.

Getting Gritty: What will happen if Jay keeps lying to Andre?

Jay, you didn't clean up the dishes like I had asked you to do.

Sorry I didn't listen mom. I'll go do it now.

So Jay, what does it mean to **care to repair?**

When I make a mistake or hurt someone's feelings I need to say sorry and what I am sorry for. Then I will discuss how I can work to prevent from making the same mistake in the future.

As you know, we all make mistakes. When your mistake hurts someone else or causes conflict you need to take responsibility and apologize in a sincere tone. Sometimes we don't want to talk about what we did wrong because we are too ashamed or worried it might make it worse.

However, if you don't apologize and talk about it (even just briefly) it can hurt your relationships. Other kids won't want to be around you. Even if they do still hang around you, they won't share their honest feelings with you and won't trust you.

It takes courage to apologize because it can feel embarrassing. When you apologize you allow people to express their own emotions and heal. If you can listen to them and learn from your mistakes it will make your relationships even stronger! It will also help you feel better, because you can forgive yourself and move forward.

www.ingramcontent.com/pod-product-compliance
Lightning Source LLC
Chambersburg PA
CBHW040036050426
42452CB00026B/86